CHANGED HEARTS, CHANGED LIVES

God's Love at Work Through Asia-Pacific Nazarenes

PAT JOHNSTON

Nazarene Publishing House
Kansas City, Missouri

Copyright 1994
by Nazarene Publishing House

ISBN: 083-411-5239

Printed in the
United States of America

Cover Design: Crandall Vail

10 9 8 7 6 5 4 3 2 1

CONTENTS

Preface   9

Who's the Guilty Party?
Papua New Guinea   13

The Journey Home
The Philippines   16

It Was for Life
Australia, Papua New Guinea   20

A Life-Changing Invitation
Myanmar (Burma)   31

Reading, Writing, and Religion
Papua New Guinea   36

A Family Endeavor
New Zealand   44

Transformed by a Dream
South Korea   46

God Honors Obedience
Papua New Guinea   48

The Most Valuable Treasure
Australia   50

Don't Feed the Evil Spirits
Thailand   53

The Extraordinary Bookseller
Papua New Guinea   56

It Has to Be Personal!
Samoa   60

Home Bible Study Dividend
Indonesia   64

God Answers a Wife's Prayers
Papua New Guinea   66

Your Testimony Counts!
  Hong Kong   68
In Times of Trouble
  The Philippines   71
Neighborhood Outreach Works!
  Australia   74
First Fruit
  Papua New Guinea   77

Pat Johnston and her husband, Gordon, have been in missionary service since 1968, when they were assigned to Beirut, Lebanon. From 1976 to 1981 they served in Amman, Jordan, and have worked on the Papua New Guinea field since 1981.

Mrs. Johnston earned a bachelor's degree in elementary education from Pasadena College (now Point Loma Nazarene College) in 1962 and a master's degree in education from California State University at Los Angeles in 1967. During her college years at Pasadena, she met her husband; at that time, he was serving as an assistant pastor at the church pastored by her father, Joe Stockett. The couple were married in 1963. They have four children.

The author has served a number of years as the Church of the Nazarene's director of publications in Papua New Guinea. In 1990 she became an ordained deacon in the denomination.

PREFACE

The Asia-Pacific Region covers one-fourth of the globe from north to south. It is a geographical area eight times the size of the continental United States. From Samoa in the east to Myanmar (Burma) in the west, it stretches out almost 7,000 miles. From Japan in the north to New Zealand in the south, it is approximately the same distance. The Church of the Nazarene is established in 14 countries with 29 districts. The 154 missionaries serve alongside 625 national pastors.

Political systems of the region include democracy, socialism, and communism. Many languages and hundreds of dialects are spoken in the region, with Nazarenes worshiping in 45 different languages every Sunday. Predominant religions include Buddhism, Islam, Catholicism, Shintoism, animism—and materialism.

To help us manage these diversities, the Lord is working to change lives for the better. Here are some of the changes that have taken place in the lives of Nazarenes in the Asia-Pacific Region.

SOUTHEASTERN ASIA

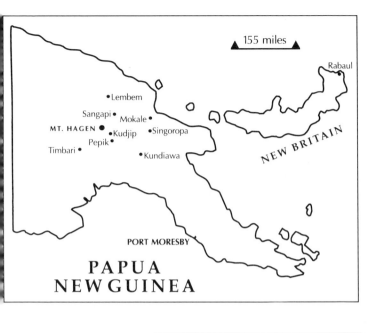

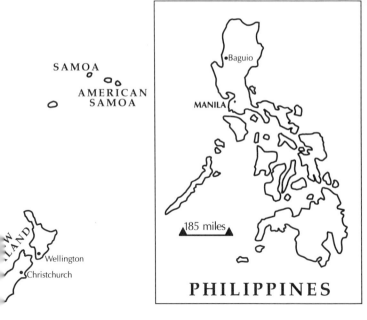

Who's the Guilty Party?

STEVEN IS A YOUNG PASTOR from Timbari in the Southern Highlands Province of Papua New Guinea. His father, Kawi, asked the Church of the Nazarene to come into that area a few years ago and even donated some of his own land so that the church could build a place of worship.

After his graduation in 1991 from the Nazarene Bible College in Papua New Guinea, Steven took a new home mission church at Muli for his first pastorate. Sometime during his first few months of pastoring, unbeknown to Steven, his father was taken to Kudjip Nazarene Hospital with a deadly combination of malaria and typhoid fever. He soon passed away.

Steven's brother was a student at the Kudjip Nazarene College of Nursing, and he notified him of their father's death. The two of them accompanied the casket back to the village for the burial.

The district superintendent wondered how

Steven, as a young pastor, would accept his father's death, because Papua New Guinea traditional culture stresses that there is always a person responsible for someone's death—especially in the case of an important man like Kawi, who was a leader of the tribe. Death could be caused by a sorcerer, someone using poison, or a witch doctor who has worked witchcraft on the dead person.

In Steven's area, a special method is used to discover who is responsible for a death. A witch doctor is summoned to the village of the deceased, takes a long piece of bamboo and somehow empowers it with the ability to levitate; and the bamboo moves in the air without support. As two men each grab an end of the levitating bamboo, it bounces and jumps around and leads the deceased one's family to the place of the guilty party. The bamboo has been known to lead a group down miles and miles of trail. As one of the men holding the bamboo lets go, it then magically points to the person responsible for the death. The accused has no recourse but to pay compensation to the family, in the form of pigs, cash, or both.

All the people of Kawi's village thought this would certainly have to be done, for he was a head man and of great importance. But Steven and his brother refused to summon the witch doctor. They carefully explained their thinking to the village: "Our father was a Christian. He had typhoid and malaria. He died, and he's in God's care now. We are not going to start this whole process of finding and accusing someone of being responsible for his death. He's gone. He's with God. We are just going to have a regular Christian funeral ceremony for him. We will not investigate his death in the traditional manner."

During the period of mourning, hundreds of people attended the four big funeral services held for Kawi. Many people were touched by the gospel as they came to pay their respects, for Steven and his brother had the opportunity to witness and preach the gospel to all of them.

It wasn't long until a delegation from Undi-ahu village, a short distance from Timbari, came to visit with Steven's family. "We have been watching you," they shared. "We have seen that the gospel has changed your lives. You haven't tried to use traditional methods to find out who caused your father's death. You haven't used witchcraft or sorcery to blame another tribe or village and get compensation for his death. We believe that the gospel is really working in your lives. We want the Church of the Nazarene to come to our village, and we are gathering timber and materials to build a new church. The gospel has changed your attitudes and actions. We want this experience too."

Yes, Steven was filled with sorrow at his father's death. But God used his Christian witness and that of his brother to open new doors for the gospel during that time of mourning. Steven's faith has been enlarged, and he continues to preach the gospel in the jungle highlands of Papua New Guinea, for he knows personally its power to change the lives of those it touches.

The Journey Home

*T*HE PRAYER OF MANY FILIPINOS is that the Lord will help them emigrate to the United States. This story tells of the Lord's working to bring Dick Umayam *back* to the Philippines!

Dick and his wife, Lorna, were brought up Catholic, but neither they nor their families had a personal relationship with the Lord. Much of their time was spent gambling. In fact, Lorna learned how to gamble in order to spend more time with Dick and her family. But she did not enjoy it, and she often asked herself, "Is this all life has to offer?"

Catholics in the Philippines have a custom of passing a black rosary from house to house. The Umayams had received the rosary, and the time had come for them to pass this special rosary on to their neighbor. Much to their surprise, the neighbor refused to take it by saying, "We don't believe." She invited Lorna to come to a Bible study in her home. Lorna attended and even held Bible studies in her own home for two years. Still, she was not satisfied with her life.

Dick and Lorna decided the answer to her unrest would be to move to the United States. But a visa was issued only to Dick. It was decided that he would go while Lorna and the three children stayed in the Philippines. Just before he left, he and Lorna spent a holiday in Baguio. Lorna was impressed by the missionary family who lived there and the Christian spirit she felt. She decided she would find a job teaching English in Baguio and moved there with the three children after Dick left.

The Lord provided them a home with a Christian landlady in Baguio. This had an immediate affect on Lorna, for while painting her new home, she found a tract. She read it and was immediately convicted, confessing her sins on the spot. She committed herself to the Lord and determined to find out more about Him. She enrolled her children in a Christian school, and they also accepted Christ because of the training they were receiving at school. Immediately, letters began to fly to Dick in the States, telling about the family's newfound relationship with God.

Lorna was not only writing to Dick; she was also writing her Christian friends in the States and encouraging them to invite Dick to church. Finally, in March 1989, a former missionary to the Philippines got in contact with Dick and invited him to a fast-food restaurant for a meal. Dick heard the way of salvation explained during that hamburger meal and accepted the Lord. The prayers of his wife and children were answered.

Dick began to attend a series of weekly Bible studies but did not attend a worship service. Finally, in September 1990, Christian friends of the Umayams were given visas to the States. They knew about a Filipino worship service in Los Angeles they wanted to attend. Lorna's first request was that they find Dick and take him to church with them. The friends came to Dick's house on Sunday morning to call the pastor in order to get directions to the church. They didn't know Los Angeles well enough to follow the instructions, so Dick spoke to the pastor. He asked Dick if he would mind bringing the couple to church. "And by the way," the pastor asked, "what are you doing?"

"I'm going to do my laundry," he replied.

The pastor then responded, "Are you doing that first before God?"

This was a very strong question in the Filipino language. It pierced Dick's heart, and the Holy Spirit immediately convicted him. So he joined his friends and went to his first church service in America.

He attended the church for two Sundays but shared that he didn't really appreciate the sermons. However, on his third Sunday, while singing songs of worship and praise, the tears began to stream from his eyes. He was embarrassed and put on his sunglasses, hoping no one would notice—but he truly felt the presence of the Lord.

In December, Dick attended a revival service and committed his life to the Lord. After his conversion he strongly felt the need to learn more about God. He made inquiries about seminaries and master's programs in the States, but nothing opened up. Then his Nazarene pastor told him, "We have a Nazarene theological seminary in the Philippines. Go home and study there!"

He called Lorna and asked her to go to the seminary in Manila, inquire about an application form, and take a good look at the place since this might be her new home. He knew he needed to study full-time if he went to seminary, and he had no job prospects. He decided to trust in God. He would put his welfare and that of his family in God's hands.

Lorna responded to Dick's request and traveled from Baguio to Manila to speak with the dean of the seminary. Not only did Dick qualify for entrance to seminary, but they were also looking for an English teacher—and Lorna met all their qualifications for the job! They could live in staff housing on campus, and the financial needs of the family would be met!

In 1991 Lorna and Dick moved to the seminary—he as a student and she as a professor. The family was reunited. Accepting the Lord as their Savior has brought many changes in their lives, but God has been showing them His greatness, and they are leaving their future in His hands.

It Was for Life

*A*USTRALIAN-BORN Margaret Robson Bromley served as a missionary for the Church of the Nazarene in Papua New Guinea for the better part of 30 years. She was converted at an interdenominational youth camp when she was a high school student. While in nurse's training she became dissatisfied with her up-and-down religious experience. "I believed God had something better for me, and I searched the Scriptures," she said. "I was sanctified at my bedside. Several months later I came in contact with the Church of the Nazarene and soon became a member."

She shared, "Just two days after I was saved, the Lord gave me a definite call to the mission field. At first I thought it would be South America. But then Sidney and Wanda Knox came through Sydney, Australia, while I was attending the Nazarene Bible College [now known as Nazarene Theological College] there, and it was because of their lives and their testimony that I knew I was to go to New Guinea, as it was then known. God also confirmed this call to New Guinea in my personal devotions."

Margaret finished her preparations for missionary service and was appointed to Papua New Guinea on October 7, 1961; she arrived on the field one month later on November 7. She was met by the missionary staff: Wallace and Mona White and Wanda Knox at Kudjip, and William Bromley, who had been stationed as a pioneer missionary in the Jimi Valley in 1960.

Margaret had met Will at an Australian district assembly before coming to Papua New Guinea, but they were just friends. Neither had any intention of starting a more serious relationship once she was on the field. She laughingly shares that the first thing she did after she met Will was hold his hand! He had an infected finger, and she treated it, because she was the district assembly nurse.

Kudjip Station was situated in the beautiful Wahgi Valley in the highlands of Papua New Guinea. At the time of Margaret's arrival, the clinic consisted of a building with a large veranda. Outpatients were treated on the veranda during the day, and an inside room was used for examinations and emergencies. Another room served as a pharmacy, and a fourth held a dental chair. Margaret confesses that after approximately three hours of instruction on extracting teeth, she was supposedly ready to add that task to her list of medical responsibilities!

On one of Margaret's first days on the job, a man was brought in with a badly cut hand. His injury actually called for the skill of a surgeon, but none was available. Margaret told fellow missionary Wallace White she just couldn't tackle the job. He reminded her that she needed to do her best, though, and added, "You're it! I'll stand by real close here and encourage you."

Sometime in the middle of the suturing procedure she looked up to find Wallace gone. He explained later that he had indeed been willing to stand by her—but his stomach hadn't cooperated! Nevertheless, his words of challenge had helped Margaret get the job done.

Margaret and Will began to develop a relationship, but it wasn't easy with Margaret working full-time at Kudjip Nazarene Hospital and Will being a three-day walk away in the Jimi Valley. Margaret declared, "The Lord just worked it out." The couple began simply by visiting when Will would come to the station; they didn't even write to each other until about eight months later—when they realized they were interested in each other.

The courtship proceded in Papua New Guinea style, meaning that they always had an audience wherever they went. They would visit in Wanda's or the Whites' home or sometimes catch a few moments of conversation when Will came to turn on the generator behind Margaret's house.

One day Will attended the wedding of two missionaries at another mission station. After his return to Kudjip, he described that wedding to Margaret—and then popped the question. Margaret later confessed that she knew she was genuinely interested in marriage before he asked her, but after answering "Yes," she thought, What have I done?

Will remained in Papua New Guinea for just a few months, and then returned to England and Scotland for a six-month furlough. That definitely made it a courtship by letter. The wedding would be in Australia, with Margaret's mother taking care of most of the arrangements. Margaret had ordered her wedding dress from a Montgomery Ward mail-order catalog and had it sent to Papua New Guinea, where she lovingly tucked it into a suitcase to carry with her to Australia.

While sitting in the Port Moresby airport on the way to Australia for her wedding, Margaret just happened to notice a man walking by carrying her suitcase. She asked him what he was doing, and he replied, "We don't know whose suitcase this is, so we are taking it off the flight." That suitcase held only Margaret's artifacts, but an identical suitcase held the wedding dress! Fearing that the twin suitcase might be misdirected as well, she frantically asked where it was. "Oh, we don't know," came the answer. "It might have been sent back to the highlands or on to Townsville, Australia." With this unresolved dilemma it was a tense trip; but when she arrived in Sydney, she was relieved to see that both suitcases had arrived.

Margaret and Will were married at College Church on the Nazarene Bible College campus in Sydney September 7, 1963. They had a one-week honeymoon and then held deputation services

23

up the eastern coast of Australia on their way back to Papua New Guinea.

Upon their return, Margaret and Will moved to Singoropa, the mission station in the Jimi Valley where Will had begun his work. Margaret was assigned to run a health dispensary in Singoropa that was built by offerings from the Australia District. She also ran "well-baby" clinics in the surrounding villages. Will had started the Singoropa Primary School before they were married, and he continued to teach in it with a Papua New Guinea helper.

The couple were thrilled when Margaret found out she was expecting their first child. She told us she had the typical textbook pregnancy some nurses experience—that is, everything went wrong! Dr. Dudley Powers, who was stationed at Kudjip, would fly to the Tabibuga grass airstrip and then ride a motorcycle to Singoropa Station to check on her progress.

As the time grew closer for Margaret to give birth, the doctors and the local Australian official, called the kiap, decided she should be moved to the hospital at Kudjip Station. A missionary from another denomination had recently given birth away from medical help and had died because of complications. It was the wet season. Torrential rains fell daily, and the clouds hung low against the towering mountains, so the small airstrip at Tabibuga was often unusable. A close watch was kept on the weather, and on the first good clear day Margaret was flown to Kudjip in a small Mission Aviation Fellowship plane.

Margaret rested at Kudjip for three weeks and then flew to Goroka for another two-week wait at the government-based hospital. Will joined her a week before the baby was born, and Margaret's mother came from Australia to be with her too. A son was born to Margaret and Will April 27, 1966. Will had always wanted to call his son John, and Margaret wanted him named after Will, so that's how John William got his name.

Just before Margaret and Will took 18-month-old John back to Australia for furlough in 1967, revival arrived in the Jimi Valley. Will had been preaching and working there for seven years without a convert. The revival started when Alu, one of the head men of the area, came to Will and said he wanted to become a Christian. In typical Papua New Guinea fashion, other people followed his lead. One of those was Duka, who often helped around the Bromley house. Soon Duka's mother and sister accepted the Lord. Not too many weeks had passed when Duka's father stood up in church and said, "I've watched the change in my wife and my son and my daughter since they became Christians. If Jesus can make that difference in their lives, I want Him in mine." That young boy is now the pastor of the Church of the Nazarene in Singoropa and also serves as zone pastor in the Jimi Valley. His three brothers are also Christians, including Phillip, who works in the finance office at Kudjip Nazarene Hospital.

Other men are also pastoring because of the

Bromleys' efforts. Pastor Kol Kina is the last young man Will and Margaret sent to the Nazarene Bible College. Pastor Kunum worked at Singoropa Station as a young man. Pastor Alu used to help Margaret in her garden. Pastor Ap accompanied Will to the Jimi Valley the very first time Will walked in—and then stayed to help establish the work there. He now is the pastor of his home church at Tun, a few miles away from Kudjip. Tarp Goma, a teacher at the Nazarene Bible College, is also a product of their ministry. As a young boy, he was present on the day Will arrived to set up his tent in the Jimi Valley. Margaret and Will's dedication and sacrifice continue to bear fruit.

The Bromleys' work as a team did not last long. John was less than three years old when Will died of a massive heart attack in March 1969. The days following his death were especially difficult ones for Margaret. How do you explain to a three-year-old that his daddy won't be coming home? John didn't understand what had happened and was upset when he caught his mother crying and would begin to cry himself and call for his daddy. He couldn't comprehend what it meant when Margaret said, "He can't come now, John. He's in heaven."

Will's beautiful flower garden had been a source of delight to him, and John used to enjoy pulling weeds and putting fertilizer on the flowers with his daddy. The Pidgin English word for fertilizer is "medicine." Finally, Margaret thought to tell John that his daddy was working in heaven's flower gardens.

One day John asked Margaret, "Does Daddy need medicine any more in heaven?"

"No," she replied, "Daddy doesn't need medicine any more in heaven. He's completely well."

"I'm not talking about medicine for Daddy," John retorted. "I'm talking about medicine for the flowers!" Thinking of his daddy working in heaven's flower gardens seemed to give John the peace he needed in regard to his father's absence at home.

John was a sweet child, and Margaret found a great deal of solace in him. His funny antics helped ease her pain. He frequently listened to his mother speaking to Kudjip on the two-way radio. Margaret would pick up the handpiece and say, "Papa Victor, Papa Victor," which was the Kudjip call signal. One day John picked up the handpiece and spoke, "Papa God, Papa God." With childlike innocence he presumed you could talk to God, as well as Kudjip, on the radio. He is now married and lives in Australia, preparing to be a Missionary Aviation Fellowship pilot.

Margaret bore not only all the responsibilities of a single parent but also that of being the only missionary at Singoropa Station. She took care of the many medical needs and found time in between to drive her vehicle on the rutted roads to pick up coffee for the people and take it to the airstrip, where it would be flown to Mount Hagen and sold for cash. She often would come home in the late afternoon and work in the garden until dark.

A year after Will's death, Margaret felt released from the Jimi Valley with the arrival of other missionary staff. She and John transferred to Kudjip, where Margaret continued to use her nurse's training in a ministry of healing. She taught in the college of nursing and supervised "well-baby" clinics in the surrounding area. The move to Kudjip was good for John, because Margaret did not want him to be raised in a woman's world. The missionary "uncles" there treated him as their own son.

In November 1984, Margaret took a leave of absence for health reasons and returned to Brisbane, Australia. But instead of thinking about retirement, she got involved in setting up the new Nazarene Health Center at Sangapi, situated in the Middle Ramu District high in the Schrader Mountain Range. Will Bromley had done the first two patrols in the area in 1964 and 1965. His recounting of those treks had made these people very special to Margaret, and although she had never been able to visit the area, she had loved and prayed for them.

After her return to Australia, Margaret never lost her burden for Sangapi. When her health improved, she requested that she be allowed to return to Papua New Guinea if there was a vacancy at Sangapi for a missionary nurse. She was asked to come and fill this spot and arrived in Sangapi to take over the health center on May 31, 1988. The health center building was beautiful, but it was still Spartan. There were no beds or mattresses for patients because the ones intended for Sangapi were stolen from the government storehouse. Margaret did her best to gather equipment and supplies for the health center.

During Margaret's four years at Sangapi, the staff increased to three community health workers and two registered nurses. Two nurses regularly went on patrol to hold "well-baby," prenatal, and family planning clinics. The other staff stayed at the health center.

Basic health care continues to be a need in the Middle Ramu area of Papua New Guinea. Malaria accompanied by parasites often causes death in children. Cold mountain streams are located far from the homes; they are not always clean and often cause infection and disease. Since all goods must be flown into the area, items necessary for cleanliness, such as soap, are expensive, and little cash is available. Crops don't grow well in the high altitude, so malnutrition is present. Margaret's prayer was that, even if she couldn't bring about complete healing for all her patients, they would at least have a chance to accept the Lord before they died.

Margaret retired in 1992 and says she did see improvement in the people's attitudes toward health care. More mothers were coming to the health center instead of delivering their babies out in the bush. Patients were being brought to the health center earlier in the course of a disease, so not as many were dying. Warren and Jean Neal, both nurses, were assigned to Sangapi to continue the medical ministry there after Margaret's departure.

Margaret never dreamed how the Lord would change her life when, as a young woman, she became a Christian. She became a wife, a mother, and a missionary nurse and teacher who served God faithfully with her whole heart. We can thank God for this woman of courage, who was so willing to give of herself to the people of Papua New Guinea.

☐ MYANMAR (BURMA)

A Life-Changing Invitation

REV. ROBIN SEIA never dreamed of all the changes that would take place in his life when that night, at age 17, he accepted a Christian friend's invitation to attend church. Robin was raised in a devout Buddhist family in Burma (now Myanmar) and had no interest whatsoever in converting to Christianity. He just went to the church service to please his friend. The two young men sat on the back pew and listened to a sermon on the love of God. "I didn't care that much about his message," Robin shared later.

The next evening his friend pressed him to attend another service. The message was from John 3:16. Robin testified, "I understood for the first time from this message that Christ came to the world to save sinners. God loved us so much that He let His son die for us."

At the close of the message, the preacher asked everyone to bow their heads and pray. "I didn't want to pray," Robin revealed. "I was a

Buddhist. But the people on my right were praying and the people on my left were praying, and I didn't want to disturb them. So I bowed my head and began to pray. Then the Spirit of God began to deal with me in a marvelous way. I felt the love of God flood my heart, and I heard the Spirit say, 'Christ has done this for you.' I didn't know anything about salvation or sanctification. I just knew that Christ loved me."

With encouragement from his Christian friend, Robin began to study the Bible and pray every day. He explains, "I avoided going to the Buddhist temple by always making up excuses. I told my family I was a new man. I did not tell them I was a Christian, for to do so would have meant expulsion from my family and relatives and community."

Robin felt Christ becoming more and more important to him each day. His walk with the Lord became his whole life. Finally, he couldn't hide it any more. He told his mother that he was a Christian. She did her best to persuade him to forget his new faith. And she said, "Whatever you do, don't tell your dad!"

Somehow Robin's father heard that he had become a Christian. He confronted him immediately. "Are you a Christian?" he asked.

"Yes," Robin responded. "I cannot hide it anymore. Christ loved us so much that he died on the cross of Calvary. He even died for you, Dad. He loves you too."

Robin's father responded in anger. He insisted that Robin leave the house at once. He was forbidden to visit his family or relatives, so he went to live with a Christian friend. Up to this point his walk with the Lord had been an easy, happy one. Now he discovered that even during the hard times he still had peace of mind and heart.

The trauma of the separation of his family caused Robin to cry out to the Lord in prayer. "What am I going to do?" he asked.

God's reply was so comforting: "The One who called you out is faithful."

So Robin continued to live by faith. He gave his life completely to the Lord. He preached when he had the opportunity and did door-to-door evangelism, telling people about the love of Christ. He began to feel God's call to full-time ministry.

After three months of prayer, Robin's mother and father became Christians. His many prayers had been answered. He told them he needed to prepare himself for ministry by attending Bible college. In 1964, however, there were no Bible colleges in Burma. A new government had come into power, and all of the missionaries had been expelled from the country.

Robin wrote to an interdenominational Bible college in Madras, India. They replied that if he would come, he would receive a full scholarship to cover his expenses. He definitely felt that this was God's solution for his training. There was just one problem. No Burmese were allowed by the government to leave the country at this time for any reason.

Crossing the border illegally from Burma to East Pakistan (now Bangladesh) and then on to India was the only alternative. It was quite a trip. "I rode the bus to a place as close to the border as I could get," he explained. "I then struck out on foot for miles and miles through the Himalayan mountain system. The walk took seven days. I finally made it to the state of Assam. My father had given me some money, and I knew I needed to catch a train to Calcutta and then make my way south to Madras. But I spoke no Hindi or any of the other languages used in India. I prayed for the Lord to send me friends to help guide me to the school. And He did."

Upon his eventual arrival in Madras, Robin lived with a missionary for a few months in order to learn the language. Later he boarded with the other students. Robin stayed at the Bible college for five years. He did evangelistic work, and was persecuted many times for his Christian testimony.

It was in Madras that Robin first heard about the Church of the Nazarene. He read some Nazarene Publishing House books, and they touched him. I would like this kind of a church in my life, he thought.

Many churches invited Robin to work with them in India after he finished Bible school. But he knew there were few Christians living in Burma, and the people needed to hear the gospel. He felt the Spirit leading him to return to his own people. A few years later, while studying at Fuller Theological Seminary in Pasadena, California, Robin attended and later joined the Church of the Nazarene. Upon returning to Burma, he opened the work of the Church of the Nazarene in his own country.

What a saga! Robin was willing to give up family relationships for the Lord. He traveled to a foreign country and learned a new language in order to attend Bible college. He studied in yet another foreign country and came face-to-face with the Church of the Nazarene. Because of his willingness to obey the Spirit's leading, no matter what the cost, the Church of the Nazarene is established today in Myanmar.

Reading, Writing, and Religion

*A*NDREW DIDN'T KNOW ANYTHING about the Church of the Nazarene. All he knew was that there was an elementary school in the Wahgi Valley near his village of Pepik, situated 5,500 feet above sea level in the highlands of Papua New Guinea. That school was at Kudjip and was run by the Church of the Nazarene.

Not very many of his friends attended school. Most of them would spend their days with their fathers preparing ground for gardens, carrying firewood or water for their mothers from the river to their thatched huts, or practicing with their slingshots by pelting banana trees with stones. His mother and father did not care if he went to school, but Andrew wanted to learn to read and write. School subjects were not taught in Kuma, the language of his mother, or Boiken, the Sepik language of his father. He would have to learn English in order to be educated.

Andrew's mother and father were not Christians. They didn't have a Bible or understand that Jesus loved them. Andrew was their first-born son; and because they wanted him to be happy, they found the money to pay the small school fee and sent Andrew off to kindergarten at Kudjip in February 1970.

The school was a considerable distance from Andrew's house. "It was a long journey, so I had to leave my home early in the morning in order to complete the two-hour walk to school," he said. "When school was finished, I walked the two-hour trail back to my home." The walk home was the tough one, for in the dry season the fiery sun was unbearably hot, and in the wet season the torrential rains of the tropics beat on his head and back.

The head teacher of Kudjip Primary School was missionary Marjorie Merritts. At the beginning of the school year she would tell the students that one of the requirements was to attend Sunday School. There was no Nazarene church in Pepik, so on Sunday Andrew would again wake up very early and hit the trail for the Merangal Church of the Nazarene. Andrew's mother and father did not attend Sunday School, so he made the long walk each Sunday with some of his school friends. Roll was taken, and a check would be put by his name every time he attended Sunday School class.

It was during Sunday School that Andrew first heard the story of Jesus. "I learned that Jesus was God's Son," he explained. "Christmas plays were presented every year by the Sunday School students, and these plays helped me to think about Jesus and the fact that He had come down to earth to suffer and die for the sins of the world."

Miss Marjorie did not realize how far Andrew and his friends were walking to attend Sunday School each Sunday. One morning she asked the children where their homes were located. She was surprised that some had walked the long distance from Pepik. She piled this group of children in her car and drove them to Pepik after the morning worship service over the dusty rutted track that passed as a road.

Upon their arrival, she called the parents of the children together and told them she wanted to start a Sunday School at Pepik with both the parents and the children attending! Permission was given, and a small group met outside under a large clump of bamboo each Sunday.

Attendance grew, people accepted the Lord through the teaching of the Word, and a church was organized. When Marjorie left for furlough, she asked Dr. Glenn and Ruth Irwin, who were working at Kudjip Hospital, if they would support the Pepik church. When the Irwins left for furlough they asked Marilyn Coffman, a lab technician at Kudjip Nazarene Hospital, to continue to support the church.

With the opening of Kudjip Nazarene Hospital in 1967, the missionary staff now included doctors and nurses. Irene Skea, the sister of Joyce Bartle, was working as a nurse at the hospital.

The Lord laid on her heart not only a burden for the sick but also concern for the spiritual development of the Wahgi Valley children. She began a children's club at Pepik on Thursday afternoons and called it the "Thursday Club." On other days, Andrew would mosey along home from school, climbing trees and trying to hit birds with his slingshot, chasing friends through the coffee and tea plantations, or wading in the Wahgi River. But on Thursdays he would rush home in order to attend the club.

It was at a Thursday Club meeting that 11-year-old Andrew gave his heart to the Lord. "Irene told us that Jesus didn't die just for adults," he said. "He also died for children—for us! I realized that meant me! I had never prayed at an altar before, and I wasn't really sure what to do. But I went forward and gave Jesus all of my burdens. I knew in my heart that Jesus forgave all of my sins and that I had received a new life through Him."

Andrew began to witness to his mother and father, and they could see the change in his life. They began to attend church with him. Missionaries Irene and Marilyn began to come to Andrew's house during the week to hold Bible studies and spend the night with the family. It was by the Holy Spirit's leading during these studies that Andrew's mother and father accepted the Lord.

Marilyn was a strong, straight preacher of the Word who didn't mince words. One evening she shared about the Bible's command to tithe.

Andrew clearly remembers the occasion: "She looked right straight at my Dad and asked, 'Akus, how much money do you make at the tea plantation?' '60 kina,' was his reply. 'OK, how much is 10 percent of 60 kina? That's how much you should be giving to God each fortnight.' 'Six kina,' he responded. 'That's right,' Marilyn stated. 'Pay God your tithe and He will bless you.'"

Andrew's father began to tithe, and God did begin to bless him. He continued to be promoted at work, and his salary was raised. Because of Marilyn's teaching, the church at Pepik began to tithe, God blessed the people, and the church grew.

Kudjip Primary School went through only the sixth grade. When Andrew graduated, missionary Nancy Seale invited him to attend a one-month training course for Melanesian Pidgin English teachers. There are over 850 languages spoken in Papua New Guinea, many of which still are not written. Pidgin English is used throughout the country as a trade language. Many people in the villages surrounding Andrew's home spoke Pidgin English but could not read or write it. By this time, the New Testament had been printed in Pidgin English, and the Christians wanted to be able to read and study God's Word.

Andrew worked as a Pidgin English teacher for two years, teaching the older people from the villages in his area to read. There weren't many men in the Pepik Church of the Nazarene who could read or were able to help the pastor, so Andrew became involved in leading Sunday church services and home-based weekday evening services. The Holy Spirit began to say to Andrew, "You could do the work of a pastor." The conviction that God was calling him to preach began to grow in his mind.

Many parents in Papua New Guinea are not happy to hear that their sons have felt God's call to preach. Many of them come from other church backgrounds, and they don't want their sons to leave the church into which they were born. Andrew's parents did not feel this way. Andrew shared, "My parents encouraged me to enroll in the Nazarene Bible College in order to prepare myself for the ministry." He entered in February 1980 and graduated in December 1982 with their full support during his three years there.

It was while he was a student at the Nazarene Bible College that Andrew was sanctified. He testifies, "The Holy Spirit did His second work in my life while I was at NBC. I decided that I would be obedient to anything God asked me to do. Wherever He wanted to send me, I would go, because I felt God would give me the strength and be with me."

Upon graduation, Andrew took his first pastorate at the Waramis Church in the Jimi Valley on the Highlands District. Although only about three hours away by car from his Wahgi Valley home, it took a real commitment on Andrew's part to accept the pastorate at the Waramis Church, for it was in a different tribe and a different language group. He pastored there for two years and then returned to his home for a year to arrange his marriage with Erika. She was a nurse aide at Kudjip Nazarene Hospital and a strong Christian, and he knew she would make a good pastor's wife.

Getting married in Papua New Guinea isn't a fast process. Traditionally, the fathers, uncles, and brothers of the bride and groom hold several meetings over a period of months to finalize an engagement, often with exchanges of food. For the wedding day, a large steamed dinner called a mumu—where food is cooked in pits in the ground—must be prepared. Pigs are killed and sweet potatoes and bananas are given as gifts between the two tribes. The bride price must be settled and paid by the groom's family. This includes pigs, cassowary birds, bird of paradise feathers, and cash. The bride's family also gives gifts to the groom's family.

Andrew and Erika were married at the Knox Memorial Church of the Nazarene at Kudjip Station in June 1984. They moved to Lae, where he pastored the Pidgin English congregation for three years before returning to his village and establishing a new home mission church at Tamban. The church prospered and grew. Within three years there were 59 members, and the congregation had raised enough money to build a permanent building with a cement floor and galvanized metal roof. God was blessing Andrew's commitment to preach the gospel.

Andrew testifies, "I have always believed that God has a plan for my life. I have always felt that if I was obedient, God would reveal that plan to me. I have thanked God always for the good things in my life."

In August 1992, Andrew was appointed district superintendent of the Highlands District of Papua New Guinea. He comments, "I did not feel adequate to the task. I told God I was too young, that I wasn't ready for this responsibility. But through His Holy Spirit, He let me know that this was His will for me and that He would help me and give me the strength and wisdom for the job."

How was Andrew won to the Lord and his life changed? It happened because the Nazarene Foreign Missionary Society earmarked New Guinea as a special project to celebrate its 40th anniversary in 1954. It happened because Wanda and Sydney Knox were faithful and came to Kudjip in 1955 to begin that work. It happened because the physical needs of Papua New Guineans were felt, and Kudjip Nazarene Hospital was opened in 1967 with its caring missionary staff. It happened because the training of pastors was a priority and a Nazarene Bible College was established there. It happened because caring Nazarenes throughout the world paid their General Budgets and gave the funds to establish the Church of the Nazarene in Papua New Guinea.

A Family Endeavor

MRS. DALE HEMA is a New Zealand Maori. She came to know the Lord a number of years ago in the Church of the Nazarene in the South Island city of Christchurch. After her conversion, the Lord marvelously helped her overcome an addiction to alcohol. Soon afterward, she was able to help lead her husband, Ray, to the Lord. She had a keen and enthusiastic spirit and was filled with the love of the Lord and the Holy Spirit.

Some time passed, and the Church of the Nazarene in Wainuiomata, a suburb of Wellington on the North Island, lost their pastor. Dale and Ray and their six children moved there in order to support the church as laymen. They lived in the house on the back of the church property for several years.

Ray was a construction worker. One day while working on the church building, he fell off the roof and died. Following his death, the Lord did not desert Dale and her children but continued working in their lives.

Dale felt God calling her to full-time pastoral ministry and subsequently attended the Nazarene Bible College in Brisbane, Australia, in order to prepare herself. She now pastors the Wellington Strathmore Park church. Two of her children have been called by the Lord into full-time Christian service. Her oldest son, Grant, also attended the Bible college in Australia and now pastors the Napier Church. Her daughter Jarrelle also felt called into full-time ministry. She, too, went to Australia to attend Bible college. She and her husband, also a Bible college graduate, and their son have returned to New Zealand to join Dale at Strathmore Park in a team ministry effort.

The New Zealand district superintendent says that the rest of this story has yet to be written: "Dale has a strong vision for her Maori people, who make up 10 percent of the population of New Zealand. We know of no one else who is concentrating on developing a ministry among the Maoris at this point in time. She also has a vision for planting a church in Nelson, a town on the north tip of the South Island."

Only God knows what the final result of Dale's conversion will be. Her obedience continues to win the lost to Him.

Transformed by a Dream

MR. PARK KWANG-CHUL is an outstanding and dedicated layman on the Korean Central District. His membership is in the Chunnong Church of the Nazarene in Seoul, which was among the 20 churches established during the 1991 Thrust to the Cities campaign in Seoul. His wife and two children also attend this church.

Mr. Park started attending the Church of the Nazarene in the sixth grade and continued to attend faithfully during his high school years. Just before entering college, he contracted tuberculosis. No medication for tuberculosis was then available in South Korea, so all he could do was rest. He spent his days reading his Bible, and God's Word became especially real to him.

One day as he stretched out on his bed, Mr. Park noticed the sun brightly streaming through his window. Then, as if in a dream, the sunshine was clouded with particles of dust. As he continued to watch, however, the dust particles disappeared and the sunlight became clear again. He then felt the Holy Spirit talking to him: "Your life has become soiled with sin, just as the air was filled with the dust particles. I want to cleanse you from your sin just as the air was cleansed from the dust." He had believed that a person could not live without sinning. But the Holy Spirit said, "Let me keep you from being a sinful man." At that point he gave his heart to the Lord.

Mr. Park felt that the Holy Spirit gave him a special mission and vision for his life. "You will find those who need help and support, and you will give it to them."

To him, compassionate ministries became a way of life. He has helped the needy in whatever way he can. God has given him a special sensitivity and awareness to the needs of others. His relationship with the Holy Spirit definitely changed the focus of his life.

God Honors Obedience

GRADUATE BENJAMIN SEKEYA of the Nazarene Bible College in Papua New Guinea had gone straight from graduation to a pastorate at Lembem, a village located in the Enga Province of Papua New Guinea. This was a brand-new area for the work of the Church of the Nazarene, and he was assigned to plant a new church.

Lembem was far off the main road. The people there practiced magic, sorcery, and witchcraft, and a real fear of evil spirits prevailed. The men were warlike and by tradition harbored spirits of revenge against their enemies.

Because it was a new area for the church, there was no parsonage or gardens. Traditionally in Papua New Guinea, newcomers to a village are fed from the existing village gardens until their own gardens start to produce. But this time the villagers did not respond: Only Pastor Benjamin and his family attended the Sunday morning worship services and, much to their dismay, the village people did not share their garden produce with them. They had to make do with what they could scavenge from the jungle.

After three months of foraging, the children became sick, and Pastor Benjamin's wife was discouraged and frustrated. In despair, after three days with no food, she took the children and went back to her husband's village.

In his heart, Pastor Benjamin really wanted to leave the ministry. He prayed long and hard over this and finally came to a conclusion: "God called me to the pastorate, and I cannot turn my back on this call. I will stay and work and pray and continue to do my best to bring the gospel to this new place. I will not follow my wife and children back home."

Just a short time after Pastor Benjamin made this decision, he went to church on a Sunday morning to find a crowd of people waiting and ready to hear his message. The next Sunday, an even larger crowd came to hear him preach. Revival broke out, and many turned their hearts to the Lord. The new Christians asked him to send for his family and promised that they would help feed them with their garden vegetables until his own gardens started to produce.

A thriving Nazarene church now exists in a remote area of Enga Province. God honored Benjamin's obedience.

The Most Valuable Treasure

*T*IMOTHY, A YOUNG MAN of Greek background, was converted in the Enmore Church of the Nazarene, located in the suburbs of Sydney, Australia. The Enmore Church congregation is made up of many ethnic groups, including British, Malaysian Chinese, Yugoslavian, Indian, Sri Lankan, and Greek. Three months after his conversion, Timothy met John Chung at the city train station and started talking to him about the Lord.

John was born in Malaysia and had completed his university studies in Thailand. He had come to Australia to visit his brother and overstayed his visa by three years. This made him an illegal immigrant.

John opened his heart and responded to Timothy's invitation to come to church by saying, "I was waiting at the crossroads for over 10 years for someone to come and tell me about Jesus. I thought Australia was a Christian country and that everyone believed in Jesus. Very soon I discovered that people avoid talking about Jesus here, and I don't understand why!"

Two months later, John attended a Nazarene youth camp in Melbourne. God spoke to him, and with tears in his eyes he accepted the Lord Jesus as his personal Savior. He immediately started witnessing to other people. A few weeks later, he was baptized as a testimony to his relatives and friends of his new life in Christ.

John witnessed to Elsa, his girlfriend. She was quite educated and had a Malaysian Buddhist background. She started attending the Enmore Church and gave her heart to the Lord. John's sister-in-law, who had a Muslim background, also started to attend church with her two sons. It wasn't very long until both of the boys gave their hearts to the Lord and joined the church.

The church became a rainbow with many different colors. It was a true mosaic picture where cultural differences, languages, and traditions vanished. The commandment of the Lord in Matt. 28:19-20 was being fulfilled in the church. The nations were coming to Enmore.

The Holy Spirit began to convict John about his illegal stay in Australia. He shared with Timothy, "If God wants me to go back to my country, I will. I'm happy now, for I will take Jesus with me. I didn't get rich in Australia, but I found God's greatest treasure here." John was unsuccessful in trying to legalize his presence in Australia and returned to Malaysia nine months after making his commitment to the Lord.

John was new in his faith, but he had fire in his heart for the Lord. As soon as he arrived back in Malaysia, he began to share his faith with his Buddhist relatives. Within just a few weeks, five of his relatives started attending church, and four of them gave their hearts to the Lord.

John's girlfriend, Elsa, decided to join him in Malaysia, and the two made plans for marriage.

John Chung's conversion touched and changed the Enmore Church of the Nazarene. According to the current pastor, "Our Lord has opened new horizons and given us a new vision for lost souls. There are over 50 different nationalities living in Sydney. We want to see people being saved and becoming missionaries to their own people. They can go where we cannot go. With Jesus we can cross over every barrier, every language, every culture. We want to continue to experience this at our Enmore Church."

Don't Feed the Evil Spirits

M ISS SIRIPAWN MALAKOON is a charter member of the Bangkok, Thailand, First Church of the Nazarene. She has been a Christian for many years. In her testimony she states, "Thailand is a Buddhist country. In fact, many of my countrymen say, 'To be Thai is to be a Buddhist.' When I became a Christian, my relationship with God through Jesus changed my life completely. Every aspect of my life had been touched by my Buddhist beliefs. Now many of my attitudes and actions had to change."

Many Thais are animistic. They are afraid of evil spirits, so they keep spirit houses in their front yards as places for evil spirits to stop and refresh themselves as they journey from place to place. Food offerings, incense, and small wood elephants are placed in front of the spirit houses each day in hopes that the spirits will be appeased and not bother the owners of the houses.

As a Christian, Siripawn does not believe

she needs a spirit house in her front yard. She explains this new belief by saying, "Spirit houses show respect to evil spirits and are unholy things. Now that I know and respect the one and only true God, there is no need for me to have a spirit house. I realize that God has power over evil spirits. God's power is stronger than Satan's power."

The Buddhists of Thailand also believe in reincarnation. It is extremely important to them to *tamboon:* to give special offerings to make merit for themselves in this life so that their next life cycle will be a better one. Siripawn states that there is no need for her to *tamboon.* She explains why: "Christians believe in one life on earth before going to heaven. Instead of *tamboon,* I as a Christian must offer myself as a living sacrifice and do God's will."

Many Thais think of Christianity as a foreigner's religion. Siripawn does not agree. She accepts the fact that God sent Jesus to die for all people, including Thais. "God's plan is for each person on earth to receive salvation, no matter where he or she lives," she says. "When I was born again spiritually, God cleansed me from sin. Only God has the ability to do that. I decided I wanted to live my life in a way that would bring honor to God. God helped me to begin to show His love to others."

Siripawn testifies that the Holy Spirit helps her in her everyday Christian life: "The Holy Spirit awakens me to things in God's Word that I need to know. He helps me to know when I have done something wrong, and He helps me to correct those wrongs. He teaches me how to serve God and how to witness to non-Christians in my family and in the world."

Although the country of Thailand is less than 1 percent Christian, Siripawn feels the church will grow if the Christians are strong in faith. She believes the secret of growth in Thailand is to be committed to prayer and to serving the Lord. Let us join her in prayer for the salvation of souls in Thailand.

The Extraordinary Bookseller

GOD HAS ALWAYS USED dreams and visions to communicate with man. We may not experience these as much today, because we can read God's Word, which He uses to speak to us. But what if you can't read? In Papua New Guinea, God often chooses to use more traditional methods to reveal himself to nonreaders. Tonga is a perfect example of this.

Dreams have been very significant in Tonga's life. As a young man, he had an extremely vivid dream in which he found himself approaching a big gate. Somehow he realized that this was the gate to heaven, even though he was not a Christian. On the other side of the gate everything was bright and beautiful, and he wanted to enter, so he knocked and knocked and knocked. Eventually someone called out, "Who are you?" He gave his name, "Tonga." "Sorry, your name's not here. You can't come in," was the reply.

But Tonga insisted, "I want to come in!" Again the reply was, "No." He continued to knock on the gate and just wouldn't give up. Finally, an angel came and said, "All right—I'll check to see if you're in The Book." To his surprise, Tonga's name was there, so the angel opened the gate and let him in.

It was such a beautiful place. The grass was green, the flowers were all blooming, and the water was clean. His dream faded after he had seen Jesus. But the desire to go to heaven after he died was instilled in his heart.

A few weeks later, a Mount Hagen Nazarene who worked as a policeman took his six-week vacation and returned to his village to begin a Bible study in his home. Tonga lived in this same village. He began to attend the Bible study and accepted the Lord as his Savior. The small group of believers who remained after the policeman returned to work became the nucleus for the Gara Church of the Nazarene.

Sometime later, Tonga had another vivid dream. He found himself walking along a path when, to his surprise, who should he see approaching him but Jesus? He recognized Him immediately by His long, white, flowing garment.

Jesus was carrying an item in each hand, and when He reached Tonga He held up the first item, a watch, and asked, "Do you see this watch?" "Yes." "I want you to look carefully at it and see what the time is." It was five minutes to twelve. Jesus told him, "That means that time is short, that time is running out. So what you have to do you have to do quickly."

In Jesus' other hand was a book. He handed it to Tonga and said, "This is for you." "But I don't know how to read." "That doesn't matter," Jesus responded. "I am giving it to you anyway. This is your job." The dream then faded away.

About this time the Simbu District of the Church of the Nazarene developed a book depot at the district office in order to supply books for sellers in the markets and surrounding villages. Tonga came and pleaded to be allowed to sell books. Everyone was a little skeptical about Tonga's ability to do this. His pastor had tried to teach him to read, but he seemed to have some kind of disability that made reading impossible. How was he going to keep track of stock, much less be responsible financially? But he insisted that this was the ministry Jesus had been pointing him toward in his dream. It was decided to let him try it.

At first Tonga was given books to bring back to his village to sell, but he wasn't very successful. The people didn't have much money, and the sun, dust, and rain were hard on his stock. Sometimes hecklers would come and throw his books on the ground, saying, "You're a new mission. Get out of here. We don't want you in our village."

It was decided it would be better if he tried selling books in the market of Kundiawa, the capital of Simbu Province. He would spread a sheet of plastic on the ground and put out one copy each of his stock. Tonga recognized each title by its cover and arranged his books by subject matter. He was quite successful—so much so, in fact, that the bookstore ended up buying him a wheelbarrow in which to carry his stock back and forth from the book depot at the district office each day.

Finally a spot opened for him to sell books on the main street of town, in a small opening in front of a trade store across the street from the bank. His stock grew from two small boxes and a few dollars in sales a week to average sales of $300 per week. Even though over 200,000 people live in the province, there isn't one bookstore—Christian or otherwise—and all of those in the area, no matter what their denomination, buy their Bibles and Christian literature from him.

Tonga has no adding machine and no cash register—just a jacket with a lot of pockets where he keeps his change and sales money. But at the end of the month—with sales of $1,200—he won't be off more than $1.00 and that might be because someone snitched a book. With the average cost of a book being $1.00, that's about 15,000 books a year. No one doubts that God spoke to Tonga in a way he could understand. Because Tonga was obedient, God has blessed his ministry, and in doing so, the Word has been spread throughout Kundiawa and the whole Simbu Province.

It Has to Be Personal!

*P*ENI (PENNY) TAKAUA and his wife, Talisua, were raised in a Samoan culture rich in religious tradition and atmosphere. Peni's parents expected him to attend Sunday morning and evening church services regularly, and he did. But, he shared, "Something was missing."

At age 16 one of his friends invited him to attend a Youth for Christ rally. The New Zealander who spoke had no formal training as a preacher; He simply shared how he had become a Christian and how God had changed his life. Then he stated, "If you have been attending church faithfully but you don't have the assurance that you are a child of God, that means something is missing in your life."

"Those words really hit home with me," Peni testified. "I gave my heart to the Lord that night. I knew in my heart I had that peace that I had never found from just being a religious person. I had never before given my life to God."

As Peni began this new relationship with the Lord, his desire was to get deeper into the Christian walk. He attended different international organizations in search of a place of ministry and met his wife-to-be in the Youth with a Mission organization. They used the Church of the Nazarene building in American Samoa for their wedding service.

It was at this time that Peni met missionary James Johnson. Peni related his feelings on hearing Rev. Johnson preach: "I sensed that he had a message that I had not heard in my own church."

After their marriage, Peni and Talisua returned to Western Samoa, and Peni found work as a policeman. Soon afterward, James Johnson came to Western Samoa and began a Bible study in the home where the Takauas were staying. Peni related, "I came home from work, and James saw me. He asked me, 'What are you doing in that uniform? I thought you were working for the Lord.' His words spoke to the cry of my heart.

"I explained that I was working as a policeman because I had a family to support. James' response was, 'I want you to think about attending the Samoa Nazarene Bible College [SNBC].'" Although Peni told him no that day, "He kept asking me to go to Bible college! One day I said yes just to get rid of him! But he didn't go away. And I did finally go to SNBC."

It was a hard decision for Peni to make. He was the only one in his family with any higher education, and his family expected a lot from him. His job as a policeman gave prestige to the family. They were extremely disappointed at his decision to go to SNBC and put a lot of pressure on him to forget the whole idea. But Peni revealed, "I wanted to study and know the Bible, and I wanted to be able to preach its truths."

He worked full-time and went to school part-time for a while. When his wife was able to get full-time work as a secretary at the Bible college, he gave up his job and put all his efforts into his studies, although he did pastor a church while a student at SNBC. He graduated in five years and then taught at the Bible college for three months. He was ready now for full-time ministry in the church.

Missionary James Johnson approached Peni at this time and said, "I want you to think about going to the Asia-Pacific Nazarene Theological Seminary [APNTS] in Manila, Philippines."

Peni's response didn't take any thought. "That would be too hard—I can't handle that!" was his quick reply.

But James repeated, "I really think you should go."

"What about finances?" Peni asked. "Our families are not Nazarene. They won't help us."

Again, James had the answer. "If God wants you to go, He will provide the finances."

Peni applied and was accepted at the seminary. He went to Manila without knowing what to expect. The family had a little money to live on for the first few weeks, but as Peni related, "We finally used up all our resources. We prayed and we cried. We decided that the best thing to do would be to go back home, and so we wrote James and told him we were returning to Samoa."

James answered them and encouraged them to finish at APNTS. Peni said, "We were forced to wait on the Lord and pray—and all our needs were met! This dependence on the Lord to provide our needs would never have happened in Samoa. But He has never failed us yet. The Lord is helping me, step by step. I am growing in Him in stages. I am learning to really trust Him. If I had known it was going to be this hard in Manila, I would not have come. But seeing God totally provide for our needs has totally changed me into a better Christian than I would have been if I had stayed in Samoa. I am glad that we have come to APNTS."

When Peni graduates from APNTS, he plans to return to Samoa to teach at the Samoa Nazarene Bible College and to pastor. His life has been greatly changed by his personal relationship with the Lord.

Home Bible Study Dividend

MR. SUNARNA IS PASTORING the Sonopakis, Yogyakarta, Church of the Nazarene in central Java. In his youth he did not even think about becoming a pastor, for he was not a Christian. After leaving school he began to work with one of the government ministers. When he found the Lord, he felt God's call to preach the gospel. It was not easy to leave this well-paying job with its bright future. But he stated, "If I am to answer God's call, I need to receive training." He resigned and attended the Indonesia Nazarene Bible College for four years, graduating in 1990.

While Mr. Sunarna was a student, he organized a Bible study in his simple home, starting with only two or three regular attenders. God blessed this time of sharing His Word, and attendance grew. At the time of Pastor Sunarna's graduation, a new Nazarene church was organized from the members of the Bible study. This new church continued to grow, and in just one year it was financially the second-strongest church on the district. It is now completely self-supporting.

Alabaster funds provided money for land on which to build a church building. Church members and friends have raised funds toward the structure itself. None of this would have happened if Pastor Sunarna had not responded to God's call to preach and been willing to sacrifice his future hopes and dreams in the business world.

District Superintendent Stephanus Hartogo commented, "God has really used this man to help His kingdom to grow." Following God's leading and direction is a must for all of us.

□ **PAPUA NEW GUINEA**

God Answers
a Wife's Prayers

TOL KINJIP IS AN EVANGELIST with the Church of the Nazarene in Papua New Guinea. Many souls have been won to the Lord through this dynamic preacher's ministry. But being an evangelist was certainly not his original plan.

Although Tol grew up close to Kudjip Station and the Church of the Nazarene, he knew nothing about the Lord. He was an important person in his village—a headman. He had worked as a policeman and traveled throughout the country with his job. His life as an adult was sinful. But in 1982 a revival was held in the Knox Memorial Church of the Nazarene that changed his life.

Tol attended an evening revival service out of curiosity, but the Holy Spirit met him there and convicted him of his sins. He didn't know anything about confessing his sins or being saved. He left the service with a heavy heart.

"I went home, but I couldn't sleep," he said. "I knew I was a sinner and that if I died I would go to hell. During the night I went through my house and collected all the things that were connected with my sinful ways and burned them in the open fire in the center of my home. But I still had no peace."

The next morning Tol went to the church sanctuary and prayed. That evening he again attended the revival, and when the altar was opened for payer he fell on his knees before the Lord. "I felt such a release. I knew that the Lord had forgiven me of my sins, and I was a new man."

His wife, Helen, had become a Christian while she was a student at Kudjip Primary School. He didn't know it, but she had been praying for him all those years. The Lord had heard and answered her prayers.

Tol began to work in the Knox Memorial Church. He often led the singing and supported the pastor in every way. Feeling God calling him to preach, he enrolled in 1983 at the Nazarene Bible College in Papua New Guinea. Upon his graduation in 1986 he became an evangelist and now holds revival crusades all over Papua New Guinea.

God heard the prayers of Tol's wife as she worked in the garden, planting and harvesting sweet potatoes and taro. He heard her prayers as she carried the firewood back to the thatched hut. He heard her prayers as she cooked the sweet potatoes in the ashes of the fire built in the center of her home. He heard her prayers as she raised their six children. A praying wife and a revival service changed Tol's heart and life and enabled him to become a workman for God.

Your Testimony Counts!

*L*OUISE LIEW WAS A YOUNG Hong Kong Chinese. She began her nurse's training in Hong Kong and then traveled to Scotland to study midwifery. At this time she did not have a personal experience with the Lord. In her midwifery class were Nazarene missionary nurses Donna Suttles and Janie Simler. They invited Louise to attend a revival service at a nearby Nazarene church, and it was there she found the Lord. She returned to Hong Kong in 1974 upon finishing her studies. Before she left, she told Donna and Janie, "I am going to find my church, the Church of the Nazarene, in Hong Kong."

Until 1974 there was no Church of the Nazarene in Hong Kong, but that year Jack and Natalie Holstead went to the city specifically to open the church there. In searching for the right place to begin, they looked at over 250 places and talked to many people before sensing God's definite leading to open the church in Causeway Bay.

This was the exact area where Louise and her mother lived!

Louise immediately became involved in the work of the baby church. She asked her younger brother, Benny, to attend church with her. Like many teenagers, he wasn't interested. She kept inviting him, however, and he eventually began to attend services with her. One Saturday night during an NYI meeting on the roof of the building in which the Holsteads lived, Benny gave his heart to the Lord. This is what Louise had been praying for.

About this same time, Louise began to feel God's call to preach. She went to the Nazarene Bible College in Brisbane, Australia, and finished the course. While there she suffered with cancer, but it went into remission and she returned to Hong Kong in April 1983.

In August, missionaries Bill and Becky Selvidge returned to the states for furlough, and Louise became the pastor of the second Church of the Nazarene in Hong Kong. When the Selvidges returned to Hong Kong in 1984, Louise's cancer had surfaced again, and she was very ill. She died in October of that year.

Meanwhile, Louise's brother, Benny, also felt God's call to preach. He graduated from high school and went to a Nazarene college in America, where he was a brilliant student. He completed the four-year course in just three years with all A's. He then completed a master's degree at the same school before pastoring in Toronto, Ontario, Canada, with the purpose of starting a Chinese congregation at the Rosewood Church. After four years there he began work on a doctorate in New Testament.

Louise's Christian influence did not stop with her brother, Benny. While in high school, Benny asked his classmate, Fai Chan, to attend church with him. It was at the Causeway Bay Church of the Nazarene that Fai was rooted in the Lord. He followed Benny to the States and graduated from the same Nazarene college. He then graduated from the Nazarene Theological Seminary in Kansas City and in October 1991 returned to Hong Kong to plant another new Church of the Nazarene.

Louise did not live the long life of service to the Lord that she would have chosen. But God wonderfully used her witness, and the chain of changed lives continues.

In Times of Trouble

MARK AND CORA TUBAL and their young son, Tonton, came to the Luzon Nazarene Bible College in the Philippines in 1988. Cora was a vivacious, beautiful woman. Mark was quiet and serious. They met at a secular college and married. Afterward they were converted, and Mark felt God's call to full-time ministry.

As the first term progressed, those on campus noticed that Cora seemed to be losing weight. She went to the doctor and was diagnosed with cancer—she had only six weeks to live. Those six weeks were difficult times for Mark and Cora. Not only were they dealing with Cora's imminent death, but they had the stress of Cora's non-Christian parents staying with them. Immediately upon hearing of Cora's illness, they had rushed to the house saying, "You need to reject your God and go back to worshiping the gods of our village. Only then will you be cured." Over and over, her family insisted that she denounce her Christian faith.

But Cora continued to listen to Christian tapes, read her Bible, and pray. Those visiting with her before her death say her room shone with the glory of the Lord.

Her burial place was on the mountainside of Baguio in a garden belonging to Mark's family. Mark made the crude wooden casket in which she was put to rest. Her parents refused to attend her burial service. "It's a Christian ceremony, and we refuse to be involved" was their comment.

Missionary Danny McMahon spoke at the graveside service. "If prayers could have saved her, prayers would have saved her. If tears and fasting could have saved her, she would be alive today. But God has chosen to take her home to be with Him in heaven."

Mark went to the principal's office after the ceremony and asked, "Sir, what am I going to do? Traditionally, the grandparents take the responsibility of raising small children if their mother dies. Both Cora's parents and my parents want to take Tonton to live with them. But neither of our parents are Christians. The last thing Cora said to me was, 'I want to see my baby again in heaven.' She did not want Tonton to be raised in our traditional village religion. She wanted him raised in the Christian faith."

The principal replied, "You bring Tonton to school with you. If we can't find him a baby-sitter, you can bring him to class with you." It was hard to return to their home and continue on with Bible college. Tonton missed his mother. But Mark assured him, "Your mother has gone to be with Jesus."

It was exciting to see the students and staff gather around Mark and support him in his time of need. Mark would sometimes get frustrated and come to the staff, saying, "I don't know how to raise a small boy by myself!" They encouraged him to discipline his son but to love him twice as much as he disciplined him.

Even with the responsibility of caring for his young son, Mark was able to graduate from the Luzon Nazarene Bible College. God gave him the courage and strength he needed to prepare himself to answer his call to preach God's Word. Tonton and he are certain that one day they will see Cora in heaven.

Neighborhood Outreach Works!

*B*RIAN AND JEANETTE EVILL and their two children lived in Dianella, on the outskirts of Perth, Australia. They thought of themselves as Christians and always tried to attend church on Christmas and Easter. Two doors down from them was the parsonage of Rev. Jeffrey Burgess, the pastor of the Church of the Nazarene in Dianella.

At Christmastime Brian invited the pastor to his home for a drink. The pastor declined that invitation, but in January he wandered down to the Evills' house and told them he'd love to have a cup of tea with them. It was then that Brian received his first invitation to attend the Nazarene church. Later the pastor met Brian at his business and took him out to lunch. He presented Brian with a tract that shared the way of salvation. When asked if he would like to pray the prayer of salvation, Brian responded by saying, "No, thanks!"

But the pastor did not give up. He asked Brian and his family to attend an Easter sunrise service to be held on the church grounds up on a hill. Brian had planned to attend a church service on Easter anyway, so he said, "Yes, we'll come." While sitting on the hill in the early-morning light overlooking the Darling Ranges, Brian became very aware of the presence of the Lord. The sky took on a bright, clear light that seemed to cover the earth.

Brian knew what he had to do. As soon as the service was over, he approached Pastor Burgess and said, "I'm ready to pray that prayer of salvation now." Together they went into the church sanctuary and knelt at the altar. God forgave Brian's sins, and he felt the presence of the Holy Spirit in his life from that time.

On his bedside table Brian had left the small tract that explained the way of salvation. His wife, Jeanette, picked it up and read it, and the next Sunday both she and their daughter accepted the Lord. Jeanette began teaching Sunday School and two years later was elected Sunday School superintendent. Brian served on the church board as treasurer and as chairman of the Board of Trustees. Regular attendance at church services and Bible studies became a family pattern.

Brian realized that his relationship with the Lord was changing his attitude about his business. Before his conversion, success in business was a priority with him. More success meant more money and more influence in the business. Now he began to turn his business over to the

Lord. He asked the Lord for guidance in giving and began to use his financial ability to help God's church to grow.

Brian was able to attend the International Laymen's Retreat in the United States the summer of 1991. He went from the retreat to the Asia-Pacific Regional Conference in Manila. God used these two events to heighten Brian's awareness of the importance of the ministry of the Church of the Nazarene, not just in Australia but throughout the world.

He commented, "My travels to the United States and Manila have been an eye-opener to me. The Church of the Nazarene is an international, intercultural church. Through its influence, significant changes are made in the lives of people throughout the world."

In late 1991, Brian had the opportunity to visit the Bible college in Brisbane. He was able to speak at length with president Robert Dunn about the work and objectives of the college. Upon his return to Dianella he felt the leading of the Holy Spirit to sell his business and prepare himself for ministry in the church. "I want to be fully equipped and fully qualified to do whatever the Lord asks me to do by the time I'm 55, he said. "That gives me five years." With the full support of his wife and family, his goals, ambitions, and aspirations are now to please God in everything.

First Fruit

A GROUP OF MEN SAT huddled over the dying embers of the fire built in the center of the men's house of Mokale village in a jungle deep in the Jimi Valley of Papua New Guinea's Western Highlands Province. Goma heard the rise and fall of the men's voices as they discussed the planned vengeance against their enemy tribe, the Moros. Headman Kosa suggested a full-scale tribal war against the enemy, while others preferred hiring the best sorcerer to cast a spell on them. There was much talking and excitement as the older men talked and the younger ones listened attentively.

But Goma couldn't concentrate on the war plans. His mind was full of the impending birth of his child, for his wife, Mambi, was in labor. He earnestly prayed to the tribal gods to give him a son.

Suddenly, one-half mile to the west came a shout from the woven bamboo house with the grass roof shared by Mambi and her pigs. With much rejoicing the midwife proclaimed, "Goma, you have a son to your name!"

There was utter silence as the good news spread through the men's house. A broad smile swept across Goma's face, and with a sign of relief he stated, "At last I have a son who will bear my family's name. The great Goma family will continue. Thank you, gods, for this son. I am Goma (klinkii pine tree), the fearless, and my son shall be called Tarp (being united together or standing side by side). By standing together side by side we can lead a strong and stable family and tribe, for I am one of the tribal chiefs."

Little Tarp grew up a typical bush boy. His dress consisted of a small bark belt held with woven plant fiber. Hanging from his front was a piece of tapa cloth made from the beaten inner bark of trees. A few leaves tucked in the back completed his wardrobe. He often accompanied his mother to the garden and watched as she took her digging stick and carefully removed sweet potatoes from the ground or planted sweet potato vines into a new garden plot. One day as he ran playfully ahead of his mother toward home, he got the shock of his life. "Mother," he called, "there's something strange going on at our tribal cemetery. I see a red-skinned man, some kind of a big house [a tent], and the village chiefs!"

Tarp timidly walked behind his mother, who with one hand was tightly holding the string bag full of garden produce she carried on her head as she headed straight for the spot. Sure enough, it was just as Tarp had spoken. This red-skinned man was Nazarene missionary Will Bromley, and he had come to live in the Jimi Valley. His purpose was to tell Tarp's people about Jesus Christ.

What a commotion the coming of this foreigner caused Mokale village! Soon the bush was cleared, and the Singoropa Mission Station was established. Curious onlookers came daily to stare at the man, watch his bush house being built, and hear his preaching.

Some of Tarp's favorite childhood memories are of the Sundays spent with Papa Bromley on the Singoropa Mission Station where he learned new songs and listened to the preaching. "The story of Zaccheus and the song 'Jesus Loves Me, This I Know' made a deep impression on my life and have been with me ever since," he said. "The messages were in contrast to what my people taught me. They were messages of hope, something that was sadly lacking in our tribal religion. Out of fear, we frequently made sacrifices to appease the spirits. But the God of the Bible and the Christians at Singoropa Mission Station loved us in spite of our traditions."

Tarp tells that Margaret Bromley had many occasions to treat him in the clinic she set up after her marriage to Will. "What happened to him this time?" she often asked. He clearly remembers her cleaning and bandaging a deep wound on his right arm that resulted when he slipped from a tree while climbing to get some fruit. Although he was only about six feet off the ground, his arm had hit the end of an uprighted stick and caused the injury.

A preschool was soon established at the Singoropa Mission Station, and, since it was his father's wish, Tarp attended. He didn't find it easy. The national teacher, who came from Kudjip, expected the students to obey strict school rules. This was really tough, for traditionally Papua New Guinea boys are allowed to do as they please.

But in spite of all of the difficulties in adjusting to living in a dorm with other boys and following a strange set of rules, Tarp enjoyed school. He commented, "The subjects we had in class and the activities we did out of the class were always interesting. And also the missionary was loving and kindhearted." At the end of the year Tarp was one of only two boys who had made enough academic progress to be transferred to the primary school at Kudjip.

Sending Tarp away to Kudjip was not an easy decision for his family to make. It was a three-day walk from home. He would be away for months at a time and live in another tribe and language group. It broke his mother's heart to know that her only son had to leave home and that she would be left with just his sister. There were many things about the white man's ways and religion that she did not understand, but she was willing to give Tarp the chance for education and the ability to decide his own future.

Six years of new experiences awaited Tarp at Kudjip. "I not only grew physically and mentally during those years," he said, "but also learned more about God's Word. Missionary teachers Wanda Knox, Marjorie Merritts, and Merna

Blowers were there to inspire me. During Easter and Christmas we dressed up like the people of Bible times and dramatized these two historical events. It was fun, and every year at Christmastime I would go home and tell Mom all the things I had learned about Jesus. It was partly through this sharing that my mother eventually came to know the Lord Jesus as her own personal Savior."

Not all of Tarp's school experiences were positive, and there were times he regretted coming to Kudjip. He explained, "Some of the local boys would taunt me by saying 'You Jimi bushman! Son of a wild pig! You son of the cannibals!' I was small in size and often seemed to end up the scapegoat. Yet in spite of this, I was determined to pass my classes and enter high school. I wanted my friends to know that I wasn't just a boy from the bush. I wanted them to see that I could survive the hard times."

God watched over Tarp during those growing-up years. One Christmas while home on holiday he took four small boys fishing. After several hours of fruitless effort, the hungry boys decided to check on an uncle's breadfruit tree, for it was the harvest season. A lot of ripe fruit was sighted, and as the oldest, Tarp was chosen to climb the 90-foot tree and knock down the fruit by using a long bamboo pole. It was an unforgettable experience.

"I scurried about 45 feet up the tree and found a good place to stand," he said. "With one hand I clung to the tree trunk and knocked down the breadfruit with the bamboo pole in the other hand. My eyes spotted a choice, ripe clump just a little further away. I loosened my grip around the tree trunk, intending to move a bit closer to my prize, but instead, I lost my hold and slipped and fell to the ground, hitting several branches on the way down. Fortunately for me, I landed on soft soil that had been dug up by pigs looking for earthworms and escaped with only bruises and no broken bones. Once again God was with me."

Toward the end of Tarp's primary education, the man he looked to as a father, Rev. Will Bromley, the missionary to the Jimi Valley, went home to be with Jesus. "I was profoundly affected by his death," he reflected. "My people who were in darkness heard the gospel of light through this man. We still mourn him today. He is buried among my own people, and on his grave marker is written, 'A warrior of the cross who poured out his life for God and the people of the Jimi Valley.' This statement beautifully describes him."

Because of his hard work, Tarp passed his grade six exams and was promoted to a seventh grade class a day's drive away from Kudjip at Mount Hagen High School. Tarp didn't claim to be a Christian at this time in his life. He testifies, "My life and heart were far from God, yet the Word of God was planted deep in my heart and I always felt conscious of His presence wherever I went. Even though I was still a sinner, I felt God's hand at work in my life."

Tarp arrived in Mount Hagen carrying a rice

sack with three pairs of shorts, shirts, a laplap (a skirt made of two yards of fabric and tied at the waist), and one small towel. In his pocket he had 20 Australian dollars. It wasn't much to face the world with!

At that time there was no Church of the Nazarene in Mount Hagen in which he could worship and have fellowship. It was hard for him to discipline himself to study so that he could pass his courses. Many times he got involved with the wrong crowd and was led astray by those who claimed to be his friends.

Again, Tarp was treated as a boy from the bush who was of little worth. He often was made the laughingstock of his class. His seat was the farthest away from the teacher's desk. With no encouragement and no self-esteem, he failed every one of his subjects that year.

Fortunately, it was decided that Tarp should be given one more try, and he was allowed to return when school started in January 1971. It was during this year that a big revival crusade was held at a nearby church. It was in one of those services that Tarp truly gave his life to the Lord.

His prayer went something like this: "O Lord, I am a failure. I failed You and Your people. I want to do good and live a life free from sin. Please forgive me now and strengthen me to live daily under Your protection. Amen." He testifies, "My Lord Jesus cleansed my heart from sin, and I felt His presence in my heart in a way I had never known before. God truly filled me with His peace and joy."

Tarp now had to face the fact that he needed new friends. "All of my bad companions left me when they saw that I would no longer participate in their activities," he said.

Ten years later, one of these companions repented and testified, "Tarp and I used to be good friends when we were in high school together. But then he gave his life to the Lord and broke our relationship. At first I criticized him, but this had no affect on his walk with the Lord. I thought to myself, 'Something has changed him. He is different now.' Over the years I could not get this memory of his changed life out of my mind. Today I stand here to tell you I have his Christ in my own heart."

Though very busy with his high school classes, Tarp found that Jesus gave him a hunger to learn more about His Word once he had committed his life to Him, so he enrolled in Bible correspondence courses. Periodic contact with the missionaries from Kudjip also had an impact on his life.

On Saturdays, some of the missionaries would take the Nazarene high school students to a park in Mount Hagen. They would play games, eat, and then share a Scripture portion or have a Bible study together. Tarp comments, "Contacts like this strengthened my love for God and the Nazarene people. Even though we were just a small group, they cared enough about us to come and have fellowship with us and to show us their love."

The scores of his 1971 school exams were in

complete contrast with the previous year. Thirty students in his class failed, but Tarp placed 20th and was given a place in the grade nine class the following year. Again he could see God's hand at work in his life.

In 1972, Tarp, along with many of his own tribesmen, was baptized at his home church in Singoropa. "It was a great day," he said. "Papa Bromley planted the seed, and now it was harvesttime. I felt it an honor to be baptized with my own people. From then on they recognized me as a Christian and knew that I would not participate in any activity that went against God's will. This continues to be the purpose of baptism in Papua New Guinea today."

In Papua New Guinea, students graduate from regular high school after completing 10th grade. Tarp scored high marks on his final exams and now needed to make a decision regarding further training. He sought advice from missionary Wallace White, who suggested Tarp fill out an application for national high school and complete grades 11 and 12, which would prepare him for even higher education. So Tarp submitted his application and then went back to the Jimi Valley for his school holidays.

One of Tarp's favorite pastimes was fishing in the Jimi River, sitting by its bank under the tall rain forest trees. He found the roar of the water relaxing. One day he and a friend headed for the river, never expecting what was soon to occur. "We had just begun to fish when I spotted what looked like a very good fishing spot on the other side of the river," he recounted. "Unthinkingly, and underestimating the flow of the current, I tried to swim across the swift-flowing torrent. The next thing I remembered was gulping down lots of water and panicking. I was thrown over one boulder, then another, and another, and around several more. I was washed ashore a half mile downstream, badly shaken up but with no serious injuries. Through God's grace I had escaped death."

At the end of the school break, Tarp received the surprising word that he had been accepted into one of the teaching training colleges for primary school teachers. He began this course of study but within a few months received word that he had been accepted into his first choice, the national high school in Rabaul, to complete grades 11 and 12. Even though his friends could not understand his decision, he felt that God's hand was at work in this opportunity, so he left the primary school teacher training college to attend Rabaul National High School.

Tarp made many good Christian friends at the national high school. God used this time to help him develop his leadership abilities when he became an officer in the Scripture Union group at school. He was no longer a quiet, timid bush boy. "It was God who changed me and gave me courage to be a leader and a public speaker, without fearing criticism."

During his prayer time Tarp was asking God to make it possible for a Nazarene Papua New Guinean to be able to attend the Nazarene World

Youth Conference to be held that year in Switzerland. Little did he suspect that he would figure in God's answer to that prayer. Here is how he explains his prayer was answered:

"It was 5:30 A.M. and a beautiful morning on May 1, 1974. I lay awake in my top bunk in my room situated only a few feet from the jungle's edge and listened to the noises of the creatures of the jungle welcoming a new day. Suddenly, in a vision, I saw myself standing in front of mission director Rev. Wallace White in his office at Kudjip. He looked at me with a broad smile across his face from behind the big desk where he was seated. Moving his chair, he stood up and reached out to shake hands with me. While clasping my hand, he said, 'Congratulations, Tarp! You have been chosen to represent Papua New Guinea at the Nazarene World Youth Conference in Switzerland.' He then handed me my passport and my traveler's checks.

"I was filled with joy and excitement and began to jump up and down while I held the two documents in the air. Actually I was rocking the bed, and my roommate, still asleep on the bottom bunk, kicked my mattress from below and screamed at me, 'Hey, Captain Blunt! [That was his nickname for me, for I was class captain, and in his own tribal language "Tarp" meant "blunt."] What's the matter with you? Let me sleep longer!'

"That kick brought me back to my senses. I immediately jumped to the floor and excitedly told my non-Christian roommate about my vision. After hearing this, he jumped out of his bunk and ran down the open corridor shouting at the top of his voice, 'Captain Blunt is going overseas! He had a vision a few minutes ago and I do believe him!'"

In the culture of Papua New Guinea, people frequently receive guidance and direction for their lives from dreams or visions. Tarp, too, believed his vision spoke of events to come and related, "I felt restless and excited about going overseas, even though there had been no official confirmation."

Later that week, Tarp heard his name being called over the public address system. The headmaster wanted to see him immediately. Tarp doesn't remember whether he walked or flew to the office, but soon he was at the headmaster's door. The headmaster smiled brightly, stood and shook Tarp's hand, and said, "Congratulations! Yesterday your church in Mount Hagen met and chose you to represent them at the Nazarene World Youth Conference in Switzerland. I have given you permission to be absent from your classes so that you can go. Your mission will be in contact with you to finalize your travel arrangements." It was all coming true.

Tarp's trip to Switzerland was everything he imagined it would be. Upon his return to Papua New Guinea, he spent endless hours sharing his new and fascinating experiences.

"God made it possible for me to see some of the world that He created," Tarp said. "I learned about time changes and jet lag, different kinds of cultures, strange foods, other methods of transportation, and the scope of the Church of the Nazarene and its people.

"It was during the eight-hour nonstop flight from Bombay to Rome that I saw my first sunrise from the air. We had left India at 11 P.M. and were somewhere over the Mediterranean Sea when dawn broke. It was like darkness fading away into light, a most beautiful and spectacular sight."

He met Portuguese, Mexican, Korean, American, and Canadian Nazarenes and in the process learned many new and interesting facts about Nazarene Youth International (NYI). In sharing his feelings about the conference, Tarp said, "I realized that the youth of Papua New Guinea were not alone. We belonged to an organization that was represented in 60 world areas at that time. The trip encouraged me to be faithful and to commit myself wholly to God and be prepared to do what He wanted me to do."

On the way back to Papua New Guinea, Tarp had the privilege of visiting the Luzon Nazarene Bible College at Baguio, Philippines. "My time there had a profound effect on me," he shared. He had no idea that he would one day return to the Philippines in a completely different capacity.

In 1975, during Tarp's last year at Rabaul National High School, God was moving among the students, and several gave their hearts to the Lord. Satan was hard at work, stirring up trouble and trying to discredit those who loved the Lord. Every night for months, Tarp gathered the faithful young people together for a prayer meeting out in the jungle near the dorms. One night a special prayer was made for God to pour out His Holy Spirit, and the Holy Spirit came down upon the group in a forceful and mighty way. Tarp explained that it was a happy and joyful experience that words could not express.

Tarp told how the students who had remained in the dorms reacted: "They wanted to see what all the commotion was about, so they slipped out of their beds and came out into the jungle clearing where we were praying and formed a big circle around us. After a while, the prayer meeting was brought to an orderly close, and the students left after witnessing our special experience that night." Tarp felt that this was the beginning of a new life in the Holy Spirit for him, and he sensed that positive changes would be occurring in his life during the days ahead.

After graduation, Tarp was accepted in the high school teachers' course at Goroka Teachers' College. He again was active in the student Christian Fellowship Group. While at the college, Tarp chose to take "Daniel" as a middle name, reasoning that "Many times I felt like Daniel, because I went to many places where there were no Nazarene churches, and many times I was persecuted for my faith. I was even labeled a priest for not participating in what my friends were doing. Yet, in spite of all that happened to me, my God never left me. He remained true to His Word and helped me overcome every trial."

One such trial came while Tarp was still at Goroka Teachers' College. There was a student at the Kudjip College of Nursing whom he was much interested in. He called her and arranged to meet with her during the Christmas break to discuss the possibility of marriage. They met, and it was decided that they should marry the following year after her graduation—but before the year had finished she married someone else!

Tarp had a hard time dealing with this. "I felt anger and resentment against God and asked Him why He had allowed this to happen." God's reply was so gentle: "My son, I know what is best for you. I am the one who is the Lord of your life, not you. You make the plans for your life, but I am the one who fulfills them."

After hearing this reply, Tarp quickly bowed his head in prayer. "Forgive me, O Lord, for questioning Your authority and Your right to my life. Give me strength to follow You always, even when I am hurting so much."

After graduating in 1977 with a high school teacher's diploma, Tarp taught two years on the Papua New Guinea island of New Ireland. He had the privilege of teaching young people God's Word and preaching in the local churches in nearby villages. These were good times in which he saw the devil fighting a losing battle in the lives of those who came to seek forgiveness. He then returned to the highlands so that he could be nearer his home and the Nazarene family.

During the Christmas break of 1979, Tarp

was asked to assist in a Nazarene high school youth camp. Late one night, he and three other Bible study group leaders sat around in a circle and discussed the needs they saw in the Church of the Nazarene in Papua New Guinea. The need for Papua New Guinea nationals to take up places of leadership within the church was discussed. At the end of the discussion, the four joined hands and made this covenant with the Lord: "Lord, if You call any of us here, we will resign from our jobs and come to work full-time with the church. This we promise." This covenant became a part of Tarp's Christian commitment, and it followed him as he continued to teach high school in another province.

Two years later, Tarp married Kalare, who had been one of his students in his 10th grade science class. In the highlands of Papua New Guinea there is no such thing as a free wife. Every man must pay a dowry to the girl's tribe— so his people helped him pay for his wife in the amount of $2,000, a cassowary bird, and 10 pigs.

After his wedding, Tarp continued to teach high school. But during the year the Lord reminded him of the covenant he had made during the high school youth camp. "Now is the time. I want you to quit teaching in government schools and come and help My people." He resigned at the end of the year and in 1983 joined the teaching staff of the Nazarene Bible College, located just 15 minutes down the road from Kudjip Nazarene Hospital. God had led him to a place where he would teach and prepare men and women to preach the Word of God and plant Nazarene churches throughout Papua New Guinea. God was a great enabler, and Tarp enjoyed this new job. Tarp and Kalare were eventually blessed with four children: Grace, William, Melody, and Nathan.

In 1986 Tarp faced one of the biggest spiritual battles of his life. His tribe in the Jimi were campaigning and gaining support for him to run in the 1987 national elections as a member of parliament. Though he just didn't know what to do, God responded in a most remarkable way. The Bible college had encouraged him and his family to attend the Australian Nazarene Bible College for two years, so he was out of the country during the election process. Tarp reflected on the lessons learned in Australia:

"It was truly two blessed years of learning more about God, His Word, our Nazarene heritage, and our holiness doctrine. Other useful knowledge included teaching that prepared me to face the ministry head on and fight the Christian battle to the end. One of the greatest lessons I learned is that to be entirely sanctified and live daily in the power of the Holy Spirit means to be the 'odd one out' in a materialistic and godless society. It is not the material things that exemplify our godliness. It is our daily living under God's power and our allowing ourselves to be moved by Him that shows our godliness. The Church of the Nazarene preaches a gospel that can be experienced and lived!"

Tarp returned to Papua New Guinea in 1988

and was appointed director of the Melanesian Pidgin English Nazarene Bible College, a position he still holds. Tarp comments on his position, "It is a challenging, though at times frustrating responsibility. Part of the privilege of being a leader is to accept that responsibility with all of one's shortcomings. God is still working on me and has not completed His work in me yet."

Just a few weeks before the 1989 General Assembly in Indianapolis, Tarp prayed a special prayer. "Mighty God, You have made my daily living a miracle. You know me better than I know myself. During this great assembly of Your people, my name will be on the ballot for some committees of the international church. If You see any usefulness in me, Lord, I am at Your disposal to do whatever You want to do with me in my life."

At the close of the General Assembly, a phone call came from the United States congratulating Tarp on his election to the Board of Trustees for the Asia-Pacific Nazarene Theological Seminary in Manila, Philippines, for the new quadrennium. His yearly trips to Manila for board meetings have been a pleasure and something he never dreamed would happen when, in 1974 as a high school student, he passed through there on his way home from the Nazarene World Youth Conference in Switzerland.

Tarp Daniel Goma truly is a dividend of General Budget. His life has been touched by the devotion of medical and church growth missionaries, church-sponsored schools, and Nazarene Bible colleges, all of which are supported by the paying of General Budget. But most important of all, here is a man who has listened and responded to God and the Holy Spirit's leading in his life. This truly is why the Church of the Nazarene continues sacrificially to support the cause of missions throughout the world.